WHEN
THE
WOLVES
RETURN

RON HIRSCHI

Photographs by

THOMAS D. MANGELSEN

COBBLEHILL BOOKS

Dutton/New York

When the Wolves Return

For Mike Harris, the Best of Friends!
—R.H.

For my mother, Margaret Berenice Mangelsen.
—T.M.

Library of Congress Cataloging-in-Publication Data
Hirschi, Ron.
    When the wolves return / Ron Hirschi ; photographs by Thomas D. Mangelsen.
      p.   cm.
    ISBN 0-525-65144-6
    1. Wolves—United States—Juvenile literature.   2. Predation (Biology)—
United States—Juvenile literature.   3. Wildlife reintroduction—United States—
Juvenile literature.   [1. Wolves. 2. Predatory animals.   3. Wildlife reintroduction.]
I. Mangelsen, Thomas D., ill.   II. Title.
QL737.C22H58   1995
599.74'442—dc20   94-16307   CIP   AC

Published in the United States of America by Cobblehill Books,
an affiliate of Dutton Children's Books, a division of Penguin Books USA Inc.,
375 Hudson Street, New York, New York 10014
Designed by Charlotte Staub
Printed in Hong Kong
First Edition   10 9 8 7 6 5 4 3 2 1

Gray wolf

A Challenge to the Children of America

Magnificant predators like the wolf and the great herds of animals sustaining them have disappeared throughout the history of the United States. People have damaged wolf habitat. People have killed wolves. Now, you have a chance to help the wolf return.

The wolf cannot live alone and, in this book, you will see faces of many animals that must be abundant to ensure wolf survival. Some of these animals must become prey of the wolf. That is the way of nature. That is what brings harmony on earth as the balance and the struggle goes on between plants and animals. The sun helps grasses and trees grow. Plant eaters—the herbivores like elk and deer—can only survive on this green

Mule deer. Lots of land is needed for wildlife to find winter food.

growth. And, the predators can only survive by hunting the herbivores.

One of the truths in nature is that there will always be more plants than herbivores, more herbivores than predators. It takes lots and lots of plants to feed one elk or deer. And, it takes lots and lots of these and other plant eaters to feed just one wolf or other large predator. The rarest and often most endangered animals are usually ones that are always less abundant in nature—the great wild hunters like the wolf.

Elk

Dall sheep

Gray wolf with prey

If we bring back the wolf, many places can return to a harmony, just like in times before our country was founded. Wolves will hunt the plant eaters, keeping them in a better balance with the land. Once, Native Americans were the only people to share life with wolves. They respected the predators and still had plenty of animals to hunt for their own food and other needs. Native Americans have always shared their lives with all plants and animals and we can learn from their experiences.

Please help the wolf. Help the elk and deer. Help the land and its plants. Listen to their needs and you may hear the wolf sing.

Orcas

According to Pacific Northwest Coast Indian legends, the first wolf appeared on their shores. It is said that a group of orca whales grew tired of life in the ocean. The whales were sleek and fast beneath the waves, but they wanted to try life on land. So, the orcas crawled up onto the shore, grew legs and fur, and

transformed themselves into wolves. The wolves ran as swift through the trees as orcas swam through the water.

Wolves soon spread from coast to coast. They hunted the great herds of buffalo, elk, and caribou—the same animals used as food by Indian people. At first, the wolf must have seemed

Grizzly cub threatening wolf away from carcass

frightening. Wolves are powerful and skilled hunters. But the Indians had long ago learned to respect all life created on earth. They learned to borrow what they needed from the earth without destroying all the animals, the forest, or the prairies. Their way has always been to share with the great hunters—wolf and grizzly on the land, eagle and hawk in the sky, and the orca whales of the sea.

Indians worked to keep a balance with nature in many ways. They were the first to set limits on how many fish could be caught in a river. In forests, they did not cut all the trees. We could learn from how they helped the wolf.

To make sure there would always be harmony between people and wolves, the Iroquois elected a person to sit at council meetings as a wolf representative. This person made sure the needs of wolves were considered each time a decision was made that might harm the wolf, its prey, or its home.

For many centuries, the wisdom of the Iroquois helped wolves. And, respect for the needs of the wolf and its home helped people too.

Bald eagles

Wolves need healthy forests, clean water, and large herds of elk, deer, and other animals. Saving the forest for the wolf meant clean air from the trees. Saving the rivers meant pure water to drink. Saving the prey of the wolf meant more wildlife for people too. All animals were plentiful in times of wolf abundance.

But the first European settlers did not listen to the wise council of the Iroquois. Settlers did not consider the needs of the wolf. And as the new people spread across our country, they cut down almost all the ancient forests. They polluted rivers. They shot and killed the prey of the wolf, the food of the Indians. Buffalo, elk, and prairie grouse were soon replaced by cows, sheep, and farms.

Bison

Elk

Blue grouse

Gray wolf

Even though no wolf had ever killed a person, the settlers also killed all but a very few of the wolves in America. Now, these largest of the wild dogs survive only in remote mountains and forests where they can hide from hunter's guns, where their homes are safe from the logger's axe.

The wolf has almost vanished. But now that the wolf is rare and in such danger, some people listen to their needs. Some people remember the wisdom of the Iroquois and other Native Americans. They try to find a way to live in harmony with the wolf and with the land.

When people help the wolf, they try to save its home and wildlife needed by the predators. The wolf has many needs—lots of land and lots of animals too. One wolf pack can live in an area of more than two hundred square miles and to protect these small family groups, we must protect large chunks of forest, rivers, and prairies. Then, the wolf will return from its remote hideaways.

When wolves return, many animals will share the earth with people, just as in times before our country was founded. Eagles will soar above treetops in vast wolf forests. Prairie grouse will dance out on the Great Plains. Grizzly bears will catch fish in wolf's wilderness rivers.

To survive, the wolves hunt rabbits, mice, and deer.

They hunt moose in deep winter snow.

Wolves chase elk and shaggy buffalo.

Wolves wander the banks of rivers and streams, hunting

Bald eagle

Grizzly bear fishing

Snowshoe hare

Moose

Elk

19

Beaver

Muskrat

Gray wolf

River otter

beaver and muskrat. Otters must guard their catch of fish from the hungry wolf.

Sometimes, wolves catch the weak, unwary, or sick. But for the wolf to survive, there must be many healthy animals so the herds can thrive. There must be healthy forests and prairie grasses to feed the prey and predators that wait.

Wolves need lots of room to roam, safe places to raise their young, and lots of trees where wolf prey can find a shelter too. When people protect forests for the wolf, the rarest wildflowers, plants that can cure disease, and the most endangered spotted owls will also be safe within these very last ancient woods. When we give room to one, we give room to all.

When wolves return, they will walk ocean beaches and lake shores in search of ducks, swans, and cranes. Birds that leap quickly will survive.

Wolves will stalk geese on prairie marshes. But wide wings will always fill our skies. Geese learned long ago the places where wolf cannot find their nests.

Spotted owl

Snow geese

Red-breasted merganser

Trumpeter swans

Moose with young

Just like you and me, the wolf must eat. Just like you and me, the wolf must have a home. But the wolf cannot eat so much or kill so much that no food is left for tomorrow. We are the only ones to take more than we need. We are the only ones who can give the wolf a home.

When wolves return, deer will run free. Moose will give birth to long-legged calves. But these hunted ones must beware when wolves return. With ears alert, they will grow more swift, more clever, and stronger too.

When the first wolves ran through the trees, long ago, the first people learned to share with the wild hunters that ate the deer that ate the plants that sprouted green from the land. We may have less to share, but when the wolves return, the grasses will still grow, the deer will find a home, and the moon and stars will still shine above the land still wild enough for wolves to roam.

In the night, the silence will vanish. When we listen to their needs, the wolves will sing. And their wilderness song will echo through your forests, across the prairie, and out on the tundra too. The wolf will sing as long ago when we help the wolf survive.

Gray wolf

How You Can Help the Wolf Survive

The most important thing you can do right now to help the wolf recover from centuries of problems is to write the United States Secretary of the Interior and your congressional representatives. Urge them to support all efforts to re-introduce wolves to former wolf habitat. Urge them and others to protect existing wolf populations from ongoing attempts to destroy these magnificent animals and their homes.

Write also to the following organizations, asking how you can join in their attempts to protect the wolf and its world. Help is especially needed in the next ten years within the Northern Rocky Mountains, an area being changed by increasing demands by people:

Alliance for the Wild Rockies, Box 8731, Missoula, Montana 59807

The Predator Project, Box 6733, Bozeman, Montana 59771

The Nature Conservancy of Montana, 32 South Ewing, Helena, Montana 59715

Greater Yellowstone Coalition, Box 1874, Bozeman, Montana 59715

The British Columbia Environmental Report, R.R. 1, Site 10, Chase, B.C., Canada VOE 1MO

Wolf Recovery Foundation, Box 793, Boise, Idaho 83701

Defenders of Wildlife, 1244 Nineteenth St NW, Washington, DC 20036

Afterword

The same Iroquois council that elected people to represent the wolf was also used as a model when our founders created the United States Congress. The idea that a president should be responsible to his or her followers is also based on Iroquois government. Maybe it is time to use this wise model once again and elect representatives to Congress responsible, not just to humans, but also to the wolf. Then, wildlife might return to many corners of the United States.

Wolves first vanished from eastern states as European settlers shot, trapped, and poisoned these, the largest wild dogs. People feared them even though no wolf has ever killed a person. Perhaps the fear was based on fictional stories from Europe that tell of "big bad wolves." Actually, many of these tales were meant to warn young people to beware of cruel men, not wild wolves.

Many people learned to dislike wolves when cattle and sheep replaced many of the deer, elk, buffalo, and other wildlife needed by wolf packs as prey. Without natural food, wolves turned to domestic animals to survive. Even today, cattle and sheep ranchers move their animals onto public lands to graze where elk and deer must compete for food with domestic stock. Ranchers fear that the wolves will devastate their herds and flocks if the wild predators return to these areas that rim much of the mountainous West. Conservation organizations have now established a $100,000 fund in case a wolf does eat a cow or lamb. Reimbursement for the animal is made from the fund. This money has shown local landowners that people do care about the ranching way of life. And, in a more positive spirit, the Defenders of Wildlife, a leading wolf advocacy organization has gone much further. The Defenders of Wildlife has additional funds which pay ranchers substantial amounts if wolves den on their ranchlands. As a result, more western landowners are changing their attitudes about wolves. Still, many cling to old beliefs and some people shoot them even in our national parks.

Gray wolf

Unfortunately, people seem to either hate wolves or love them. Because of the strong feelings, it is difficult to help restore the wolf. This is true even though our country was founded, in large part, with an understanding that wild animals belong to all of us and that each person owns wolves in common. In other words, you own the wolves that roam in America just as you own each and every other wild animal. With that ownership comes the right to enjoy wildlife, no matter where they live.

That the wolf has vanished from nearly every state is a sad reminder of the abuse of that ownership and responsibility we all share. But the bold and sometimes dangerous attempts to restore wolf populations (biologists helping the wolf receive death threats from those opposed to restoration) help people remember that wildlife is still important to America. And, wolves are especially important as key predators.

A key predator is one that affects populations of animals it lives with, not just those it preys upon. When wolves live in an area, prey animals are healthier and not as likely to overgraze plants. Natural balances are met because the wolf reduces populations of the plant eaters and harmony exists as fewer elk and deer devour a limited source of food. That harmony can be restored when we return wolves to our country. You can do your part by urging your congressional representatives to vote for all measures that help the wolf and other wild predators. Their future is in your hands.